SHRINES

SHRINES

IMAGES OF ITALIAN WORSHIP

PHOTOGRAPHS BY STEVEN ROTHFELD

TEXT BY FRANCES MAYES

DOUBLEDAY

NEW YORK LONDON TORONTO SYDNEY AUCKLAND

Mary who intercedes, who sallies forth with our prayers, who watches over, who suffered as all mothers suffer and more, who calms, who comforts—it's she who most often appears in shrines. She's a friend, divine but still a friend. We think of her when we wear blue and when the rosemary blooms. If God appears on earth we might hide our eyes in fear but Mary, we would invite Mary in to the table.

She seems, too, to be the most sited among the holy: at Fatima, Lourdes, Guadalupe, the black Madonna in Czestochowa—so many manifestations of her presence. We travel to those miraculous places hoping to breathe the air she breathed, to brush the caper bush where her skirts passed, hoping for miracles.

Near Ephesus stands the last home of the Virgin Mary. Almost certainly not true, the legend of the site represents a wish of ours that her last home be located. A German mystic published a book in 1841 describing her vision of Maria at Ephesus, and archeologists later found a fourth-century ruin and grave there. That the fourth century is many, many years afer Mary's time has not deterred visitors ever since. When I visited, heaving busloads emptied into the parking lot and headed to the little stone house. These pilgrims, appealing for her intercession or giving thanks for the same, have attached to a wall whatever was at hand, handkerchiefs, Kleenex, panty hose, small photos, and pieces of maps.

Another house of Maria, her birthplace in Nazareth, was transported by heavenly assistance in 1291 to Trsat in Croatia, then again was lifted in a great angelic puff in 1294 and flown to Loreto, near Ancona, where it still can be visited. Clearly, the connection of Mary and the significance of the house have deep mythic juju. The Madonna and the longing for home are seamless. And so she naturally becomes the one to station near the door or in the piazza or along the road to home.

Miracles are for the long pilgrimages, but the Maria of the household shrines is for everyday life. "Protect this house," I saw scrawled on a little card propped in a shrine on Capri. In private chapels, little family churches, roadside shrines, and bedroom altars, sometimes you find Jesus on the cross, or sometimes San Francesco, but the image of the Madonna is ubiquitous. The gas station, the Carabinieri office, the butcher's shop, the bank, the blacksmith's, the mechanic's garage—look up and there she is, often with a twig of olive branch behind her image, often next to the nudie calendar.

She has ubiquity and higher power. Type in "shrine to Mary"on a Web search and 217,000 entries pop up. She's in the air, everywhere, down to earth. She has a stare that nearly burns the metal grate she's often behind. She's not bothered by roses gone off, pigeons pausing in flight, or sun angling into her eyes. One early summer morning in Naples, I wandered around visiting Madonna shrines. I didn't follow a guidebook, and I didn't think where I was going. This is a good way to get to know the city. My only goal was to pay attention, because the shrine with the images of the Madonna is everywhere, so it's sometimes difficult to concentrate after you've seen five. Although some shrines announce themselves on the corners of important streets, most are more unobtrusive, demure, unostentatious. If they're at human level, their ledges for flowers are stuffed with plastic hydrangeas and real potted azaleas and cut gladiolus. One of my favorites housed a tomato can full of garden roses. Others have softly winking electric bulbs over them, or a humming rim of neon blue. Some are covered in frozen rivers of candle wax. A few are abandoned and you wonder why when others nearby are not. They are folk art. They are sacred. They occur at the juncture of spirituality, the impulse to create art, and the concern for everyday life. They are above all made by someone's hand, some uncle or stonemason friend. Maybe he chose the form and materials (brick vs. stone), then a discussion one night over pasta settled the matter. Lucia would buy the statue, Cecilia would mix the right color of paint, and she and Mama would paint the inside of the niche marine blue, then Don Antonio would come to consecrate it.

From that moment on, the shrine becomes a focal point that wasn't there before, a piece of architecture, yes, but not like a new door or window that wouldn't cause anyone to notice. The new shrine gets attention from the beginning and keeps getting noticed. It becomes meaningful not only to the family that constructed it, but to those who pass, including me on a June morning, peering at the curled notes and saints' cards laid among the flowers, and the metal cut-out arms and legs that someone running on an image and a prayer hoped would bring a cure.

At our house in Tuscany, we have a stone niche at the bottom of the driveway. Inside there is a Della Robbia-style Madonna and Bambino. At the first moment I saw it, I also saw Bramasole and I knew instinctively that this would be home. During the early years here, while we were clearing the abandoned land of brambles, a very solitary man used to bring flowers to the shrine every day. He wore his coat over his shoulders, even in the blast furnace heat of August, and he paid no attention to us wielding clippers and weed-whackers on the terraces above. He was on his daily mission. He took the flowers from the day before, dropped them in the ditch, swept out the shrine with the side of his hand, and propped up his new bouquet of yarrow or dog roses or poppies. After years of his visits, suddenly they stopped. No one in town seemed to know this man. He never returned and I assume he died. Our neighbor's ancient mother, too, used to visit the shrine daily. She brought her own offerings of flowers. I also began to keep a jar of roses or a handful of daffodils from the garden in the shrine. Just as the two visitors died, an odd twist of fate occurred. Readers of my books about Tuscany began to visit the house. They started to leave mementos in the shrine—coins, pine cones, wildflowers, candles, pretty rocks. Grouped photographs of each other in front of the shrine. Our neighbor, Placido, rides by on his horse and bows his head and crosses himself, In the name of the Father and the Son and the Holy Ghost. Katia comes jogging by, arms pumping a sign of the cross. Chiara, our neighbor's daughter, has taken over her grandmother's vigil. When we return after a long absence, we are certain to be welcomed home by Mary, a lighted votive, and a vase of whatever blooms from her garden that the season offers.

Most of the shrines in these splendid photographs by Steven Rothfeld also have such an ardent life. A shrine becomes a hot spot in the landscape. The shrine is so long in Italian history. The Romans had their household, as well as public shrines, for their many gods. At home, at least three were honored, Lar, the god of houses, Janus, looking in and out of the doorway, and Vesta, goddess of the hearth. Lares, tutelary deities or ancestors, watched over the house, as did Penates, other gods of the house who focused on the family's food and cupboards.

The shrines we find today are late expressions of this ancient tradition. They still enliven the lost roads, the corners of villages, and the gated entrances to towns. I have seen impromptu shrines on the dashboards of battered Fiats. All nations and cultures may have their religion's versions of shrines, but Italy must outdo them all with the variety and number of shrines. They are not only for prayer or paying respect. The shrines come from a very important human need to anchor the foundation of the *casa*, *strada*, or *città* to something divine. Walking around Naples, this came to me, and explained to me my own fascination, which I share with Steven Rothfeld. The photograph, as a piece of intense attention paid, is also a fragment of the divine. The true image hands back a truth.

Frances Mayes

SHRINES

II

13

So many saints stand under an arc
of brick or stone or painted plaster.
An arc is a part of a circle that
represents the apparent course
of a heavenly body, Sun or Moon,
Venus or Mars, suggesting the same
for Mary, saint or archangel.

19

PER GRAZIA RICEVUTA
M. B.
24. 2. 1951

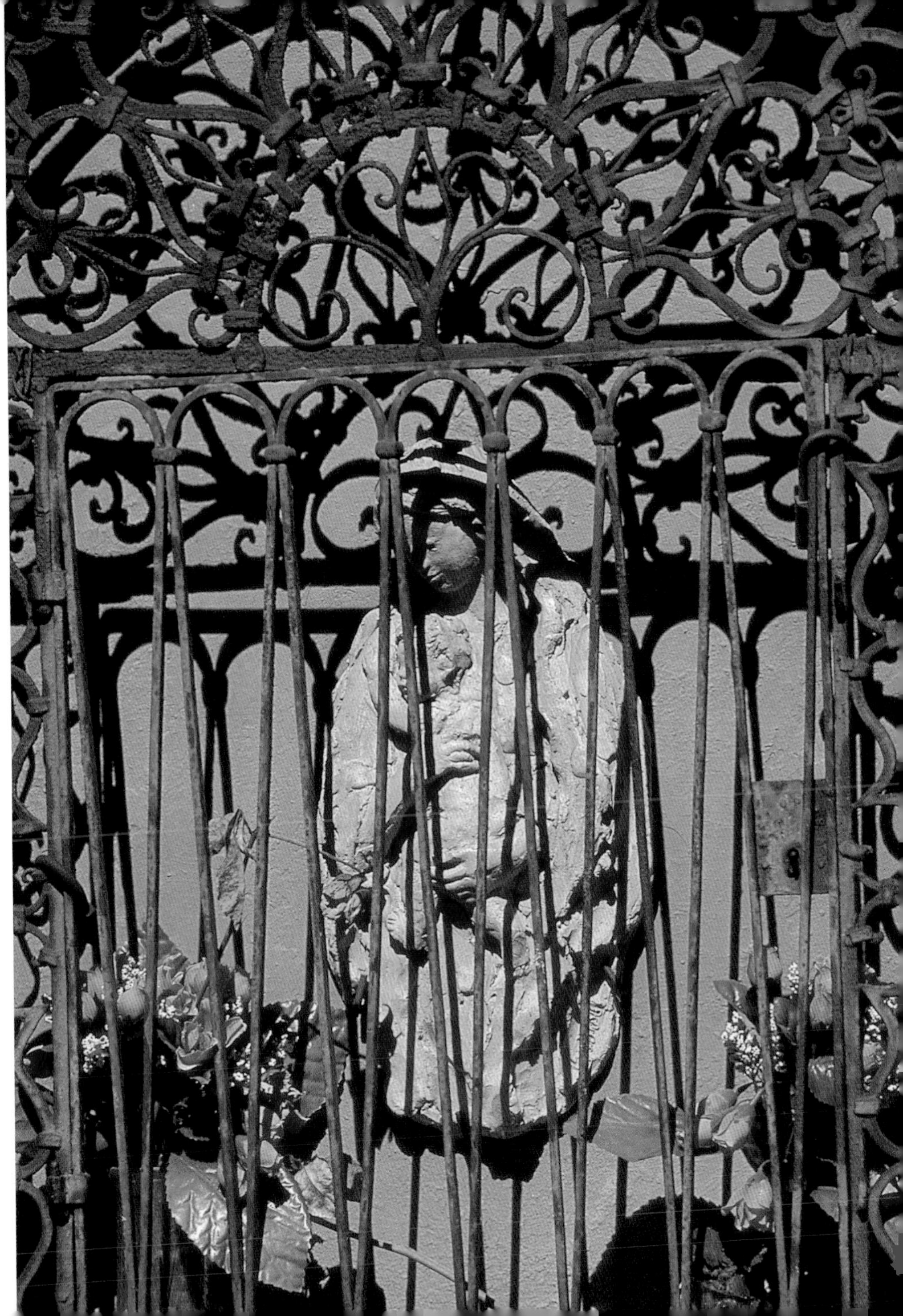

33

In a purely secular sense,
shrines punctuate the landscape.
Like cypress trees, like bell towers,
like stone walls and olive terraces,
shrines add their particular
character and depth.
Imagine Italy without them.

37

39

Of all weathers, mist is the most
spiritual. A cypress tree has majesty
on a sunny day. On a misty early
morning the cypress tree becomes
a presence and the air around it
seems protective and mysterious.
You can imagine then those who
worship trees. The mists of autumn
go with what Keats called a season
of mellow fruitfulness. If you believe
in ghosts, you'll think they ride the
mist. While fog broods, mist flits,
slips, rises, evaporates in a flash.
I've noticed that shrines seem to
attract mist. Perhaps the ions are
pulled as if magnetically. The
enshrouded shrine is a double call
to the faithful pilgrim, and even to
the most blasé atheist. This is so
because the mist is a vapor akin
to the soul, and suddenly you see
the soul materialized around a holy
image. You must stop and pay
homage, even if only until a small
breeze clears the air.

When I first drove up to Bramasole
with the agent, I got out of the car
and faced the shrine right outside
the gate. I thought then how good
it would seem to be greeted by
Mary every time I came home.
Over the years we have lived
here—fifteen now—I have loved
placing flowers in the shrine. The
postman crosses himself as
he passes by, as do joggers and
those out for an afternoon walk.
The shrine has a life of its own.

59

MATER DIVINÆ
GRATIÆ

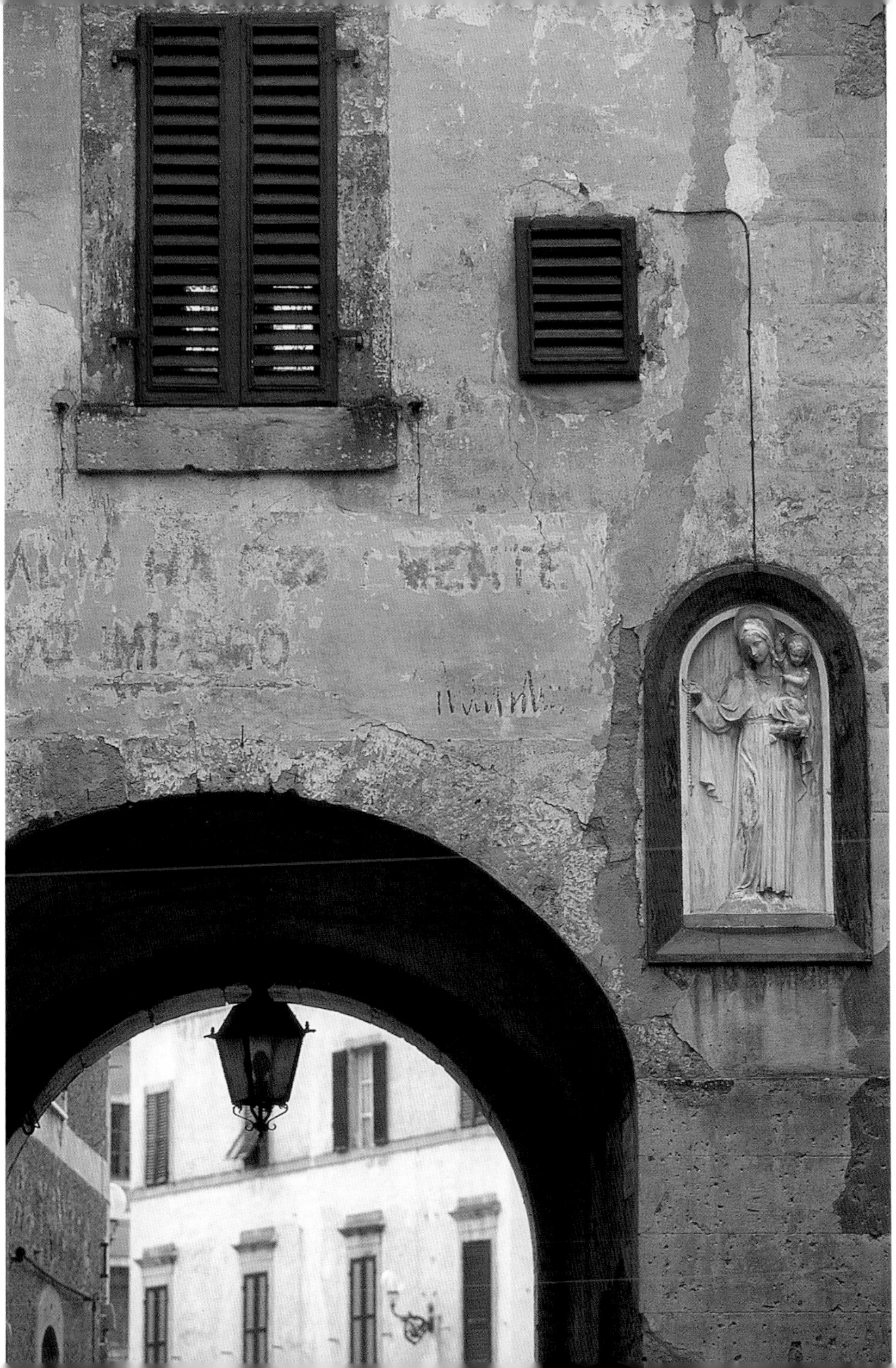

FERMATI PASSEGGERO
IL CAPO INCHINA
SALUTA DEL CIEL
LA GRAN REGINA

What's absent in these images
is as mysterious as what you see:
the shadows and gestures of those
walking by, those who have passed
the shrine so many times that it has
become a mirror in which they
can no longer see their reflections.

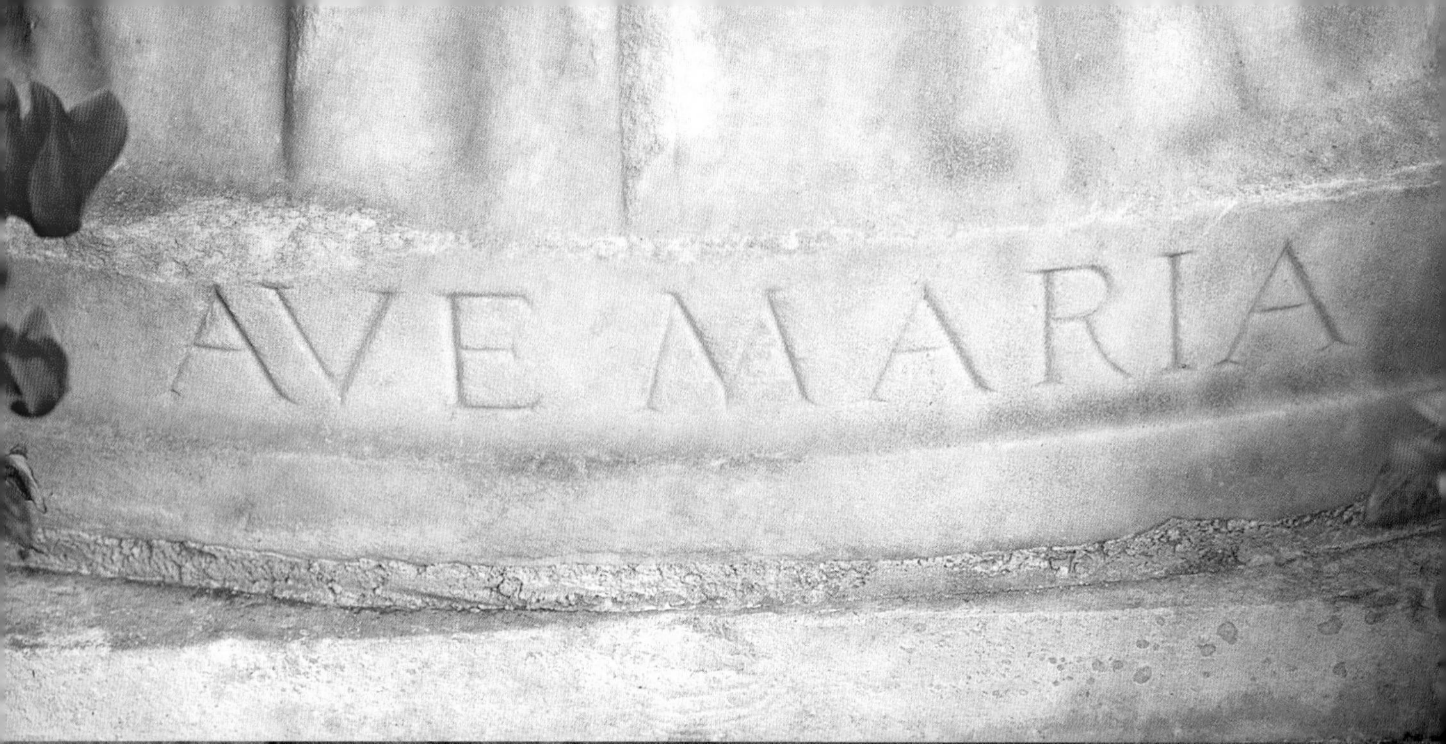
AVE MARIA

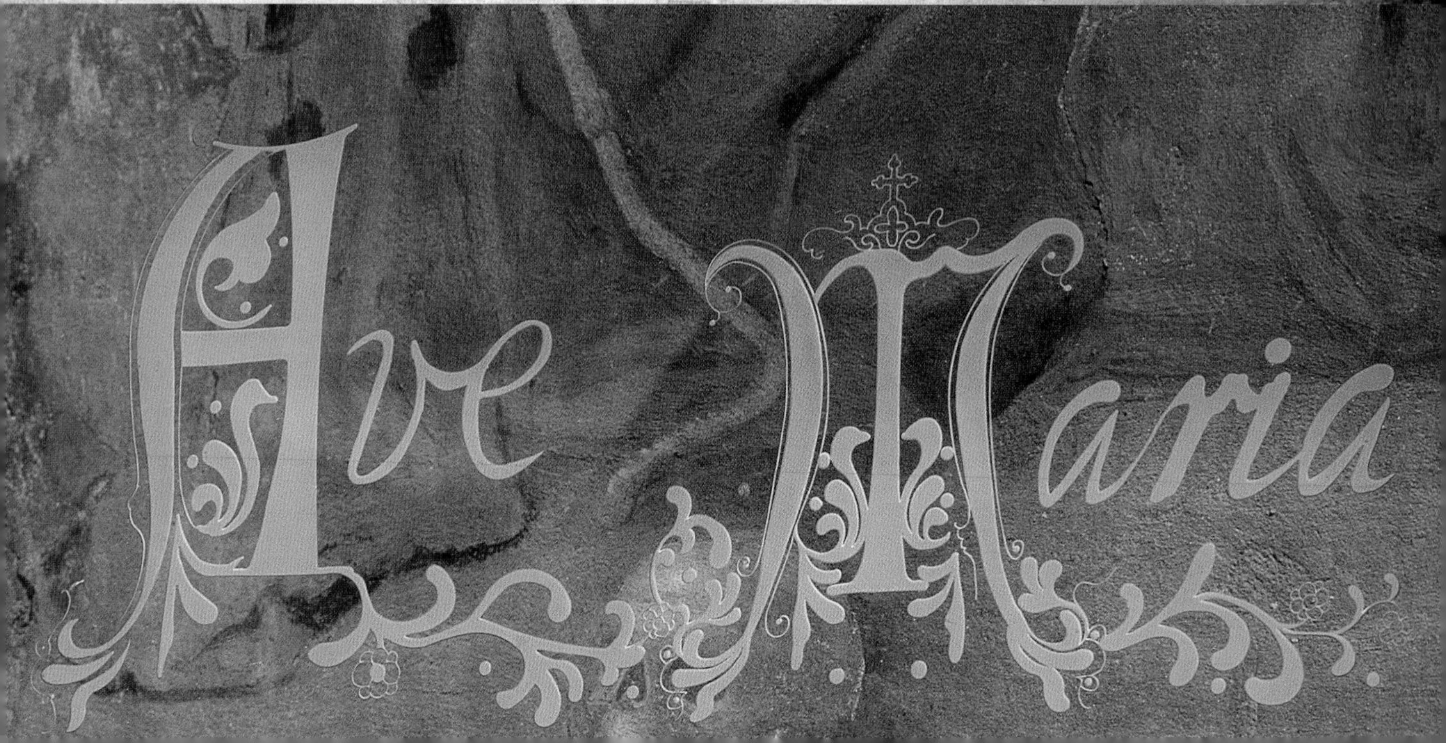
Ave Maria

VICOLO

AVE MARIA

ANNO SANTO 195

Does Maria read thoroughly
the minds of those passing, those
who ignore her, as if she were a
lamppost, a mailbox, a hotel sign?
And the minds of those who stop,
whether they're longing for a way
out of their world, or thankful that
they found a way into it?

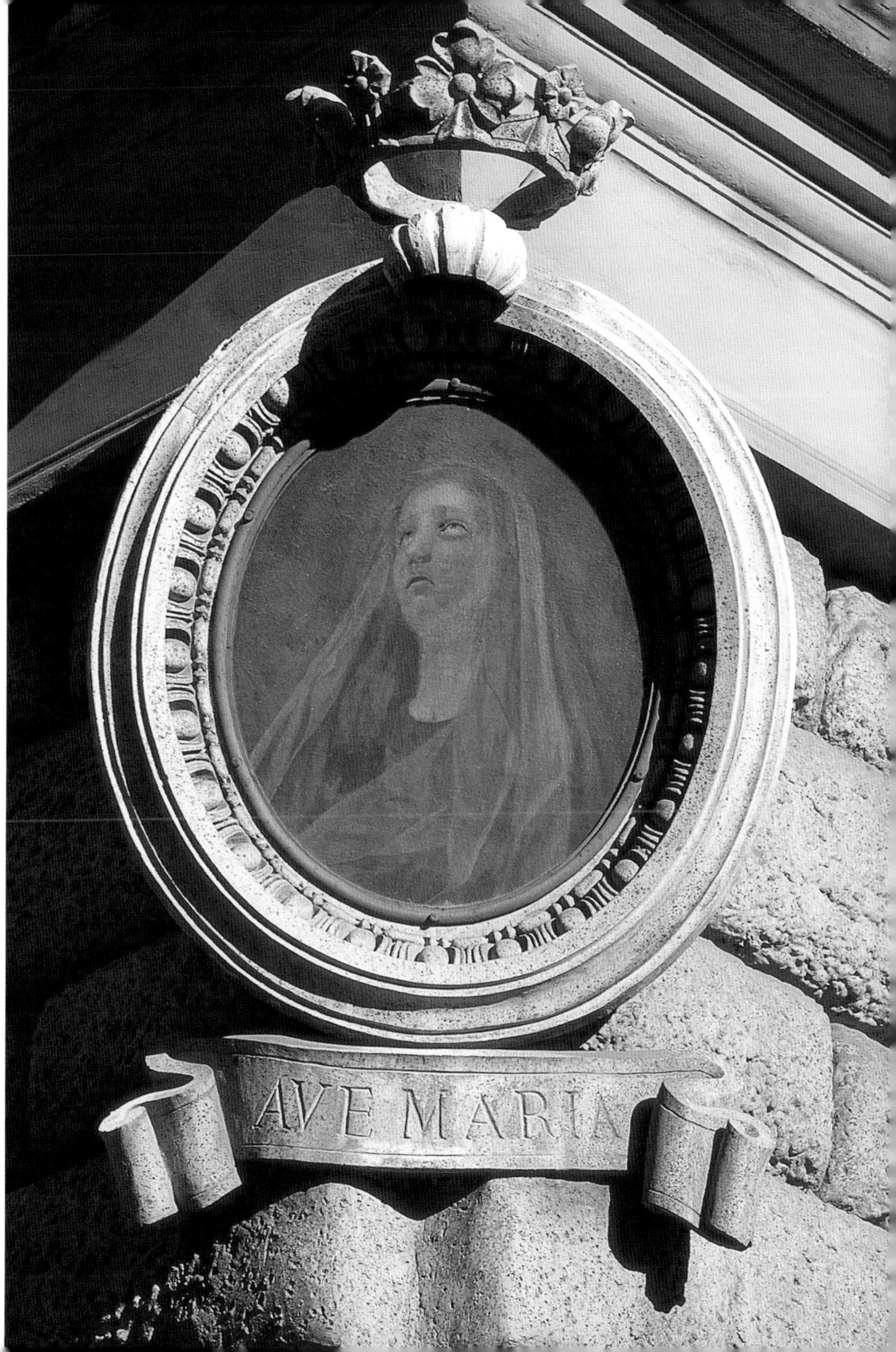
AVE MARIA

109

A shrine, unlike a santuario,
a sanctuary, isn't always
a destination point, a pilgrimage
point, but more of an object one sees
on the way to someplace else—
on the way to your neighbor's
house, the grocery store, the park.
What a pause at a shrine brings
to this moment of daily life, then,
is a sense of stasis, in the Greek sense
of "a state of standing." There's
at least a moment in the hurry
to do this and that, even if it's
a mental pause, a recognition that
the Virgin Mary or San Francesco
or an Annunciation angel is a still
point, fixed forever, while you,
temporal and human, move on,
return, move on.

AVE MATER ET VIRGO

Do they see us?
Do their eyes follow as we pass?
If I reach to touch a foot or hem
of robe, will I feel a small shock?
Is a kitschy Madonna still powerful?
Did the artist love the chalky blue?
Did he sleep the sleep of the blessed
after painting this?

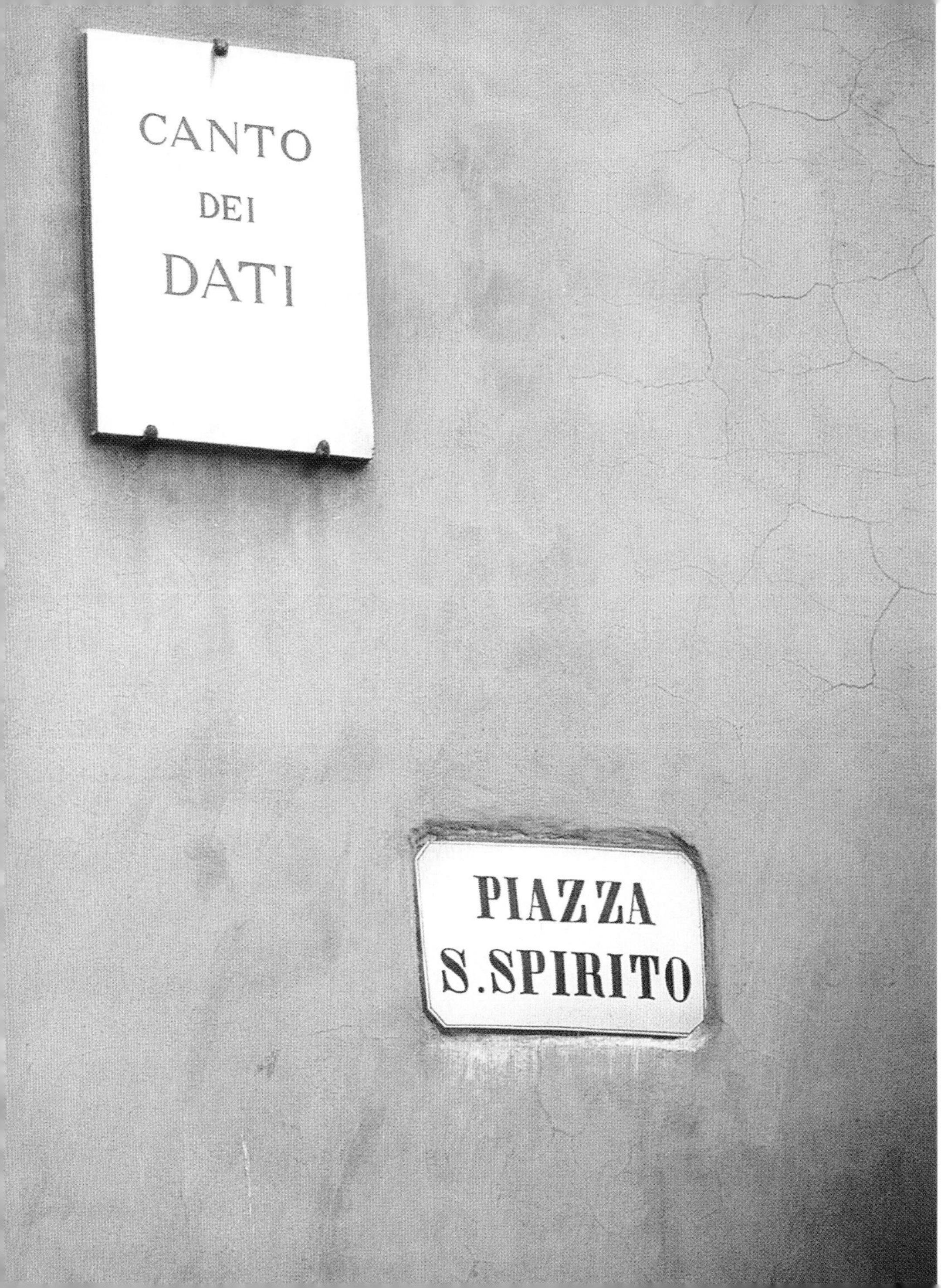
CANTO
DEI
DATI
PIAZZA
S.SPIRITO

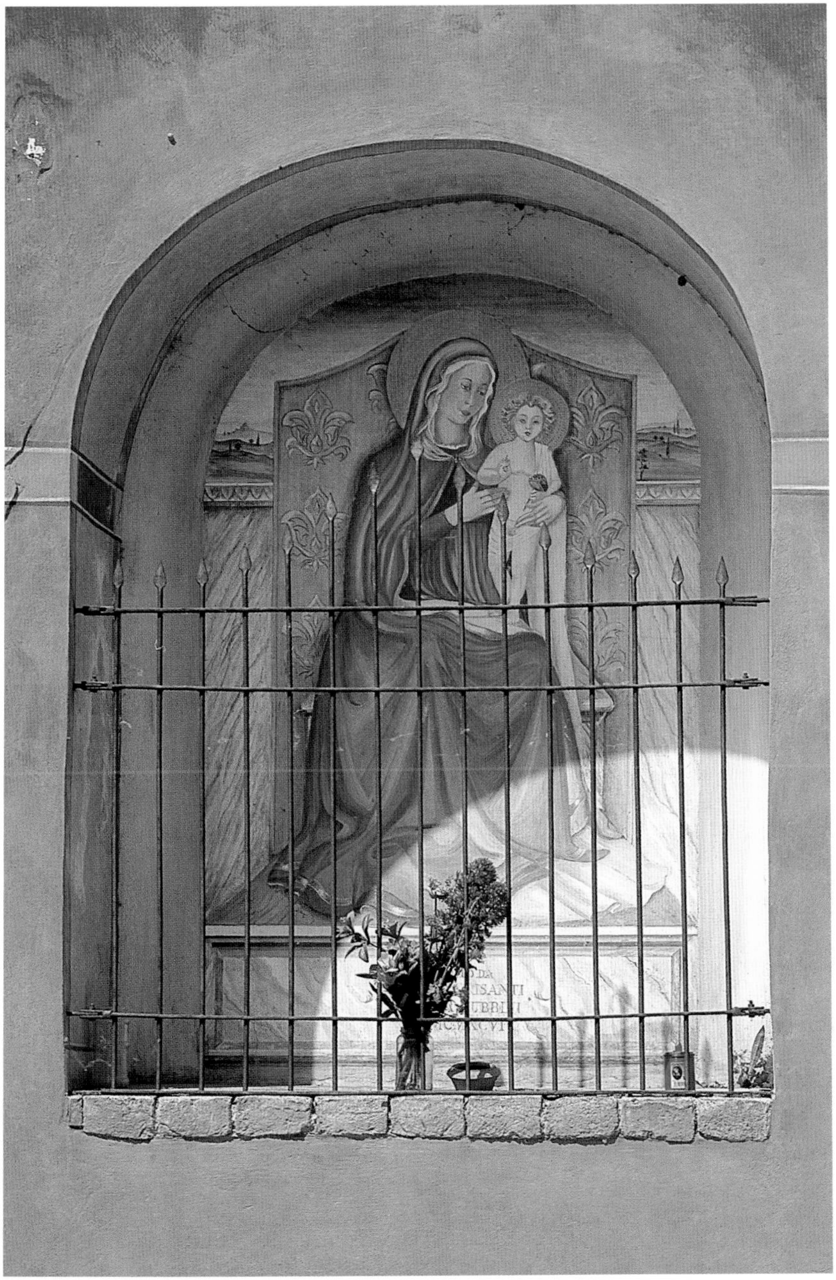

The shrine is a sacred place that draws the brave and scared, the complacent and adventurous, the free and chained, and the curious. In Cortona, beneath a neon-ringed Madonna and the statue of Santa Margherita with her attribute, a devoted dog, a small real dog often sleeps. The shrines have magnetic force, pulling to them those who need to be pulled.

VIA
DELLA CHIESA

...OSSEQUIA LA GRAN MADRE DEL SIGNORE

CHE ULIVELLI EFFIGIÒ SOMMO PITTORE

L'ANNO MDCLXVIII

INDEX
TO
SHRINE
SITES

143

PUBLISHED BY DOUBLEDAY

Photographs copyright © 2005 by Steven Rothfeld
Text copyright © 2005 by Frances Mayes

All Rights Reserved

Originally published in Italy by Mandragora, Florence, in 2005.
With editing, design, and typesetting by Monica Fintoni,
Andrea Paoletti, Paola Vannucchi.

Published in the United States by Doubleday, an imprint of
The Doubleday Broadway Publishing Group, a division of
Random House, Inc., New York.
www.doubleday.com

DOUBLEDAY and the portrayal of an anchor with a dolphin
are registered trademarks of Random House, Inc.

Library of Congress Cataloging-in-Publication Data is on file
with the Library of Congress.

ISBN-13: 978-0-385-51887-1
ISBN-10: 0-385-51887-0

PRINTED IN CHINA

10 9 8 7 6 5 4 3 2 1

FIRST U.S. EDITION